Devotions
for
Later Years

Wallace Fridy

Abingdon Press

For my wife
Frewil Culler Fridy

Devotions for Later Years

Copyright © 1991 by Abingdon Press

This book is published on recycled, acid-free paper.

ISBN 0-687-105161

MANUFACTURED IN THE UNITED STATES OF AMERICA

95 96 97 98 99 00 01 02 03 — 10 9 8 7 6 5 4 3

CONTENTS

FOREWORD

These devotional messages have a twofold purpose; namely, to be used as resource material for those responsible for leading worship services for older adult groups and for use in one's private devotions.

They have all been used in amplified form as sermons trying to speak to special needs of older adults. Of course, as with most sermons, they first spoke to the minister's own need and then were shared with his people. And it is hoped that since they have arisen out of the daily experiences of life, they may have a message for you who read them and who use them. Some of them are adapted from material which appeared in my earlier books, *Adult Devotions* and *Devotions for Adult Groups*.

At the end of each chapter are worship aids to assist the leader in holding devotional time. There are hymn and scripture suggestions, in addition to a prayer.

In one of her books, Margueritte Harmon Bro tells of someone going to an artist's studio to see a new painting. He was first guided into a dark waiting room and left for ten minutes. Then the artist himself came in and explained saying, "I knew if you came into the studio with the glare of the street in your eyes, you couldn't possibly get the color values."

This suggests to us that we need to find a time and a place where we can pull apart from the noise and glare of daily living and there find God. It may be in a chapel, a church, an attic, a secluded spot in a park. It may be in solitude or in company with others. It may be in the early morning hours, at noonday, or when the shadows have lengthened and night has come. It can be a time of inspiration when the glare and glitter of the streets are erased from our eyes and we can see life in clearer perspective. It can be a place of renewal.

These messages are sent out with the prayer that those who read them in private or who are led by them in group worship may discover help in finding the meaning of life and the strength to face it victoriously.

WALLACE FRIDY

LIFE IS A LANDSCAPING JOB

Someone has well said that life is a landscaping job. We have been given a site with contours, with possibilities, with limitations, with general outlines, many of which are beyond our control. Our job is to take this site and see what we can do with it.

Each of us is interested in getting the most out of life, in finding these years allotted to us to be fruitful and happy. But the fact is that many of us are not doing a good job of landscaping our sites. We are failing, and life is meaningless.

In Deuteronomy 30:19 we have these words: "I have set before you life and death, blessings and curses. Choose life so that you and your descendants may live." To choose life is to landscape it, to handle it, to plan it, to nourish it, to use it for good.

Well, what are you going to do with your site?

In the first place, *we must accept our sites*. We cannot say, "If I had somebody else's land, if only my soil were richer, if only I had a better view, then I'd really build and plant and landscape."

We must start with our sites as they are. They are ours to use and to cultivate. We must accept our sites. We cannot overlook the starting point. Where we are going, what we shall do, whether our dreams can ever come true—all depend upon the starting point, here and now. Our sites include many limitations. Many have inherited family responsibilities. Others have met misfortune. And many face crippling illness. These, too, we must accept as part of our site. We cannot escape what comes our way, but we must accept it as part of our lot.

In the second place, if we are to do a good job of landscaping, we must not only accept our site, but *clean off the underbrush and fill in the gullies*. This means that we must do what we can to improve our site. We must eliminate that which gets in our way.

People dissatisfied with life many times discover the cause to be sin and wrongdoing—the underbrush. From the history of the human race we cull this one note; namely, sin never paid good dividends. The weeds of life must be eliminated if fruitful plants are to grow.

Many times we wonder why religion isn't more meaningful, or why God doesn't help us, or why we are so barren spiritually. Frequently, the reason is that there are too many barriers in the way. We want to be happy, but we aren't willing to pay the price. We want to have our own way, and we don't want to give up that which we know is standing as a barrier to happy living.

Sin separates us from God, and a person who is separated from God can never find life fully satisfying. Clean off the underbrush and fill in the gullies if you would begin well on your landscaping job.

Finally, *plant and leave the rest to God.* In other words, we must do the best we can with what we have and leave the rest to God. This is all God asks. And the thing that counts is not so much what happens to us or what remnants life has left, but what we do with what we have.

Hymns: "This Is My Father's World"
"Guide Me, O Thou Great Jehovah"

Scripture: Deuteronomy 30:15-20

PRAYER

O eternal God, whose heart is filled with goodness and love for us all, whose compassion can comfort the soul in our moments of anxiety, draw us near to you as the sun lifts the waters from the sea. Heartaches cause us to stumble, but you are an ever-present God whose will is to strengthen our weakness. Let not fear, trouble, or pain lessen our devotion to you, but rather cause us to lift our eyes to the hills from where our help will come. Gird us with endurance when even to exist at all requires strength not our own. Help us to realize that even in suffering you can use us as you used the suffering of your Son to heal a broken world. Even when life seems to be slipping away, give us a consciousness of your presence and a realization that though the body may break, your love and constant care can never be taken from us. Speak to us in the lonely hours of the night when sleep will not come, and stay with us in the day even when the clouds hang low, through Jesus Christ our Lord. AMEN.

GOD'S DAY ENDS IN THE MORNING

In Genesis 1:5 we have these words: "And there was evening and there was morning, the first day." This is not the order we usually think of the day taking. Our thought is that day begins in the morning and ends in the evening, but the writer of Genesis puts the evening first. When sunset comes, we do not say that the day has begun, but rather that it is drawing to a close.

Yet throughout our Bible this thought prevails, that sunset is the beginning of the day. Throughout Jewish history this same idea is followed, and even today it is this same reckoning—that day begins at evening.

This concept roots far back beyond the Bible when the earliest tribes were nomads of the desert. In the heat of the desert sun they kept in their tents. In the cool of the evening, life could actively begin.

But does this not have more meaning than that expressed in the custom of these ancient people? Was there not in mind a deeper consideration? Does not God's day really end in the morning? Let us look at this thought—darkness is not the end but the beginning.

In the first place, out of the night came God's first creative act—namely, creation. The primary fact was darkness and mystery. It was out of this void that God created the world and all that dwells within it.

In Genesis 1:2 we read, "The earth was a formless void and darkness covered the face of the deep." Here it speaks of night out of which came day. Darkness and then light. So God's first creation was light.

The fear of the dark, of course, is rooted back in primitive man, who never knew what dangers might be lurking in the night. The little child is afraid at times of the darkness. And, too, what grown man or woman has not feared the darkness when illness was acute? The darkness made it seem more sinister, and there was longing for the breaking of the dawn.

But to know that it was out of the darkness that God created, suggests to us that God is active too in the darkness of our night. All of the universe belongs to God. There is no aspect of our experience that can be without the presence of God. "If I ascend to heaven, you are there; if I make my bed in Sheol, you are there. . . . If I say surely the darkness shall cover me, and the light around me become night . . . darkness is as light to you" (Psalm 139:8, 11-12).

It is to say that God is near in the darkness as well as the light. He is present when life walks in the darkness. Thus we believe and have faith at night, so the shadowed side of life as well as the sunny is part of the realm of faith. No trial or disaster can be so dark as to eclipse the redeeming presence of God.

In the second place, not only was it out of darkness that God created light, but out of the darkness of our experience many times comes the dawn—day begins in the evening.

It is when we are broken in spirit, when life crowds us in a corner, when we are in despair, when our human resources fail—these are often the times when light begins to break for us. It is not the end but the beginning of new life.

It is the record of human experience that out of darkness comes a new way of life. Light has come when we are more conscious of the shadows. Darkness has been for the human soul a time of meditation when life's values are weighed, when we have reached out for help beyond our own, when what really matters in life has been comprehended.

So, the day for you may have as its beginning the darkness. When you are discouraged, when life has lost its meaning, when the bottom has dropped out—these are times of darkness which can be from God's point of view and your own the beginning of the day. The end is the morning when light appears.

In the third place, we see this truth revealed in the cross, when darkness hovered over Christ. His disciples were in despair. The earth darkened at the crucifixion.

Then came the Resurrection. The day ended with the Resurrection. The cross was in reality the beginning of the day. Love broke forth on the world. The bonds of death were broken.

It suggests to us that death is not all, that in God's plan it is the real beginning of the day. God's day ends in the morning. How we need to know this!

Hymns: "Still, Still with Thee"
"Sun of My Soul"

Scripture: Genesis 1

PRAYER

Eternal God, we give you our gratitude this day for life and our privilege of living. And so teach us to number our days that we may apply our hearts unto wisdom.

We thank you that every blooming flower, every blade of grass, and every singing bird suggest to us your loveliness and beauty. Grant that as new life bursts into slumbering nature, a new spirit may arise in us today.

Prepare our minds and hearts for this hour. Make us conscious of our sins and shortcomings. Awaken us to our dependence upon you. As we think of those forces which led to the crucifixion of our Lord, help us to see in ourselves the sins which led to his death. Recall to our minds the sacrifice that was his that we may know better the height and depth and breadth of God's love. Make us to rejoice that the darkness could not hold him but that he is alive forevermore.

Be especially near to those whose pains are almost too heavy to bear. Bind up the wounds of the brokenhearted. To those facing difficult decisions, guide them to make right choices. To those confronted with temptation, give them clear heads and strong wills. Help us to be patient, to be kind in our criticisms of others, to be fair in all our dealings with others.

May our Christian witness be such that will draw others to you, will brighten the dark corners of life, and will reflect the spirit of the risen Christ, and in his name we pray. AMEN.

THE DARK NIGHT OF THE SOUL

Who of us has not faced the dark night of the soul, when the bottom seems to have dropped out, when the course ahead seems blocked? What are we to say to these low moods, these disturbing moments, these dark nights?

For the background of our thought let us turn to the experience of the prophet Jeremiah when his world was filled with darkness. Raymond Calkins in *The Romance of the Ministry* illuminates Jeremiah's experience.

Jeremiah was a young man living in Anathoth when God called him to the task of bearing a message of judgment to his own people, whom he loved. How inadequate he felt to fulfill such a summons! The more he thought about the corruption of the nation and the immorality of the people, the more depressed he became.

The whole countryside lent a hand in adding to his depression. His call had come at the low point of the year, bleak mid-winter. All around the land was barren and cold. Suddenly in the midst of his despair he lifted his eyes and beheld the sight of an almond tree breaking forth into bloom.

It was just one slender shoot, sheltered by a bank from the cold wind, but that was enough for him. The bloom of the almond in Palestine is the first harbinger of spring. For Jeremiah that flowering rod was a reminder that God was alive, that all was not lost. Yes, it became a sign of spring, a touch of color in the bleakness. The rod of the almond tree became to Jeremiah a reminder that God was alive and at work in the world; that in spite of the coldness of winter, summer was on its way. And in the strength of that assurance that God was alive and working, Jeremiah went forth to answer God's call. He went in the faith that there was an unseen power at work, that God was guiding him all along the way. The bloom of the almond became a symbol for him that remained real in the long years ahead and always drove him forward to his tasks in confidence. What does this tell us?

It tells us that when we face the dark night of our souls, we need this sign of the almond tree. We need it today. God is saying to us today as he did to Jeremiah, "No, all is not lost.

There is hope, for I am at work! I am still in command. Even though the clouds of discouragement hang low they shall be blown away, and sunshine shall come again to bathe the earth with its healing power." Yes, the affairs of life can be bad, but they are not all bad. Always in life there is the shoot of the almond tree, the promise of new life and energy beneath what seems to be barrenness.

However dark may appear the winter, let us never forget that springtime is not far off. When we become discouraged, let us never forget that God's energies are at work silently but powerfully for righteousness and peace. After we have surveyed the field, let us not leave out of our calculations the spiritual forces that join hands with us in the task.

Hymns: "A Mighty Fortress Is Our God"
"Lead On, O King Eternal"

Scripture: Isaiah 40:1-11; Jeremiah 1:1-11

PRAYER

O God, whose love has never let us go and beyond whose brooding care we cannot drift, we would quiet our souls in your presence and rest ourselves in the confidence of your sustaining strength, that the peace of God which surpasses all understanding may guard our hearts and thoughts.

Through countless channels you seek our lives, at many doors you stand and knock. We wait now for your still small voice which can change our fear to faith and our cowardice to courage.

Grant to us faith in you, that in the face of life's illness and trials we may share Jesus' trustful, confident mind, and be freed from the cares which destroy us. Grant us his unfaltering belief in your goodness, that whether pain or joy be our lot, we may still know ourselves to be upheld in your strength. In his name we pray. AMEN.

DOING THE BEST WITH WHAT YOU HAVE

Many there are today who are living with inward discord brought about by a tension between what they are and what they long to be. Each one of us has faced a situation where on one side are aligned things as they are—our capacities, our abilities—and on the other what we are hoping they will eventually be. On the one hand is the actual self and on the other the vision of the ideal. Oftentimes the gap between these two positions is so great that inwardly we feel frustrated. Dreams become too lofty ever to have a chance of being achieved.

Now to be sure it is good to have dreams, but to dream too high is sometimes as dangerous as to dream too low. When what we are and what we hope to be face each other with no chance of meeting, then an inward civil war begins.

This may sound rather strange to be cautioning anyone to watch the heights of ambition, for so many are dreaming too low today. Many never aspire to any one thing that is greater than what they have at the moment. Surely we need to dare to look upward. But to dream too high may become in itself self-defeating when the summit is never approached. To hold high ambitions is a vital part of the development of personality, but this happy faculty, if misdirected, can tear life to pieces.

As we face this matter of starting with life as it is, we find that *we must accept ourselves*. We must face frankly our abilities as well as the limitations which life has given us.

This principle of self-acceptance can be applied in every realm of life. A peach tree will not produce apples. Tomatoes will not bear beans or corn. These things were not intended to produce other than what they are. Of course botanists can perform wonders in grafting and cross breeding, but the major functions of plant life remain the same.

So, in these lives of ours God does not intend for us to do the impossible. And just because one can become an eminent physician does not mean that that person is fulfilling a greater function in the eyes of God than one who daily does, to the best of his abilities, some other task that he is more suited for. Some can do many things and do them well; others can do only a few, or perhaps one thing well.

No one has had a more undesirable beginning than George Washington Carver, who just before his death was called one of the world's greatest agricultural chemists. He was born in a slave home, stolen by slave thieves, and taken to live in a white man's home without mother or father. He was equipped with a frail body. Yet from such a start he rose to a place of fame and was the recipient of hundreds of honors. This great man surely had to start with life's remainders, but he did the best he could with what he had.

What are you doing with what you have? This is the most important question we face today. The little boy on the hillside had only five loaves and two fish, but they fed the multitude. With them alone he could do little, but in cooperation with Christ wonders were achieved. The world is full of people who have traveled far on little baggage—not only people who gain fame, but humble folk whose names will never be recorded in the annals of history but will be written indelibly in God's book of life.

And it is never too late to start over again. In A. J. Cronin's book *Keys of the Kingdom,* the Chinese gardener Fu was distressed over what a storm did to his flowers. But Father Chisholm said: "Let us be of good cheer, Fu. The damage is not irreparable." "My plantings are lost," Fu gloomily replied. "We shall have to begin all over again." Then Father Chisholm responded: "That is life . . . to begin when everything is lost!"

Hymns: "Lord, Speak to Me, That I May Speak"
　　　　"Take My Life, and Let It Be"

Scripture: Proverbs 3:1-10

PRAYER

O God, we come to you empty-handed, for all we possess comes from you. We stand before you as having nothing except what you have provided.

We are small, but you are great;
We are weak, but you are strong;
We are ignorant, but you are wise;

We are finite, but you are infinite;
We are revengeful, but you are forgiving;
We are sinful, but you are pure.
   O God, how dependent we are upon you. You are our hope,
our strength, and our life. AMEN.

LANDING ON BROKEN PIECES

Acts 27 gives a classic account of a storm at sea. Paul, you remember, is a prisoner being taken to Rome. The storm arises between Crete and Malta, and Paul had advised against sailing in the late fall. He was an experienced traveler on both land and sea and knew the perils of going to sea when the winds would be at their worst. His advice was not taken. The storm arose and threatened all on board. But Paul had a vision and with confidence told them that they would all reach shore, to have courage. And so they did.

This is a parable about life. Storms arise on our journey and most of us are forced to land on some broken piece and finish our course. We all have our storms—dreams broken, plans changed, lives altered. Disappointment in love, the loss of a job, the death of a loved one, the curtailment of education, a crippling disease—such we face today. And they leave for us broken pieces on which we are to journey.

Let us look at this truth.

In the first place, *we should do all that we can to avoid the storms.* When Paul advised against sailing, he was bringing his common sense to bear upon the situation. He did not advise that they go rashly out to sea in defiance of the seasonal storms. He rather advised that they use common sense, profit by their knowledge of the weather, and try to avoid the storms if possible.

This is the first step we all should take if we are wise. We should guard our health without being too anxious. We should not place ourselves deliberately in the presence of disease without some real reason or purpose. If our family is in danger, steps should be taken to prevent harm. If there is discord, everything should be done to ward off catastrophe. Or if harm has already been done, the situation must be altered if it possibly can.

Someone has well said that this business of rising above the circumstances of life, of sailing against adverse winds does not begin with endurance. It rather begins with an intelligent effort to change the circumstances and to prevent their occurrence.

This is what Paul was trying to do—to change his plans but he failed. We, too, are not always successful in altering an unwanted situation or of controlling circumstances. Many times after we have done the best that we could in a given situation, we are faced with strong winds against us. What are we to do?

This leads to a second thought: namely, *to continue to hope and not give up in despair.* Regardless of how bad a situation may be, we need not despair. This is what Paul did. He told all on board to take heart. They were words which had as their source a vision which Paul had during the night. He lived with the assurance that God's will would be done. He was confident that it meant that he should reach Rome and witness there.

We cannot explain just what his vision was, but we do know that Paul lived a "two-dimensional" life—plans of his own which gave way to plans that God had for his life. He lived under the direction of God and was guided by God's wisdom.

It is a great thing to believe that your life is in the hands of God and that God is working out a divine purpose through you. It is a greater thing to give your life over to that purpose and know that nothing can happen to you that need cause despair.

This means finally, that when we land on life's broken pieces, *with God's help we can reach the shore.* It means that we are to accept the wreckage after the storm and try through God's help to use it for good. It is to pick up the broken pieces of life and fit them into a lovely mosaic. And it is the Christian faith that proclaims the Good News that there is a merciful God whose plans are not completed here, who offers us strength to withstand life's disappointments, and who helps us triumph over them. For most of us the fact is that if we are to reach the shore, we have to do so on life's broken pieces.

Hymns: "Holy, Holy, Holy"
    "I Need Thee Every Hour"

Scripture: Acts 27:33-44

PRAYER

O eternal One, we come again this day asking for your ear and voice, praying that you would listen to what we have to say and tell us what you would have us know. You have spoken to us in sorrow and in joy, in the stillness of the night and at noonday, when the clouds were hanging low and when the sun had swept them away. Help us, we pray, to hold steady even when all sense of your presence is gone. Too often we are pushed about by the cares of this world; poise and peace are far from us. We have felt the pull of your love as it continually reaches out for us, but the adversities of life take hold upon us. When the night is dark, the storm roaring, and your light cannot be seen nor your voice heard, may our faith be so grounded that nothing can shake us from following your will. O God, grant that it may ever be so. In Christ's name we pray. AMEN.

LIVE A DAY AT A TIME

Let us use these words "live a day at a time" as a principle which we all need to heed. It is suggested to us in some lines from one of the ten most popular hymns of all times, "Lead, Kindly Light."

> Keep Thou my feet;
> I do not ask to see the distant scene;
> One step enough for me.

Here one can find the secret for mastering life.

And how we need to find it today. The psalmist was thinking of this principle when he wrote, "This is the day which the Lord hath made; we will rejoice and be glad in it." One day at a time. The psalmist is saying this is all we have. It is all we can manage. It is all we need.

Let us look at this principle.

In the first place, a day at a time is all we have. It is foolish to worry about tomorrow, for we do not know we will have it to live. Only today confronts us.

In the second place, a day at a time is not only all we have, but it is all we can manage. Jesus was thinking of this when he said, "Do not worry about tomorrow, for tomorrow will bring worries of its own. Today's trouble is enough for today" (Matthew 6:34). He is saying to take it as it comes. It is all we can manage.

Finally, one day at a time is not only all we have, all we can manage, but it is all we need. If the main purpose of life is to find God and be found by God, then one day is all we need. Let us not let any day pass without coming close to God.

You say how can I approach one so good, so perfect? He asks so much of us. He speaks of perfection. All that God asks of us is that we take one step and follow the light we have toward him, and then further light will break forth on our pathway.

"This is the day which the Lord hath made; let us rejoice and be glad in it." Live one day at a time, for it is all we have, all we can manage, and all we need.

Hymns: "Dear Lord and Father of Mankind"
"Savior, Like a Shepherd Lead Us"

Scripture: Luke 14:16-24

PRAYER

Most gracious God, Father of our Lord Jesus Christ, our Father and the Father of all people everywhere, your greatness is beyond the conception of our minds. Your concern for your children exceeds the care of our earthly parents. We pause today acknowledging our unworthiness and asking you to judge us by your great mercy and not according to our merits.

Coming into your holy presence makes us conscious of our feebleness and sinfulness, for in your light our lives are blighted with scars. Yet we would remember the promise of your Son, who assured us of forgiveness to those who repent and return to you.

> Forgive us for doubting moments when your promises lie hidden in our minds.
>
> Forgive us for selfish ambitions unbecoming to your servants.
>
> Forgive us for jealousies which canker the soul.
>
> Forgive us for lack of faith when darkness makes us afraid.
>
> Forgive us our slowness to see the virtues of others and our quickness to see their faults.

Awaken us to our manifold needs. Help us remember that what led Jesus to the cross is like the evil we find in ourselves. Drive us to our knees in penitence for all our failures and raise us up as your new followers, through Jesus Christ. Amen.

A HITCHING POST OR A GUIDEPOST?

Leslie Weatherhead, in his book *When the Lamp Flickers*, has a sentence which reads: "He does not wave to us from the past; He beckons us from the future." Of course, this does not intend to minimize the importance of the historical setting out of which Christianity arose. It is firmly established historically and geographically. Our faith is grounded not on myth, but on fact and history.

To say, however, that Jesus does not wave to us from the past but beckons to us from the future is to say that not only is he a historical person who moved across the stage of history, saying and doing wonderful things, setting for us a marvelous example to follow, and then ascending into heaven; but also that Christianity is not a hitching post which holds down, but rather a guidepost pointing the way. It is faith which has to do with the present and the future.

You remember Jesus' words in the last chapter of Matthew when he said, "Remember, I am with you always, to the end of the age." This is the central fact of our faith and one which needs re-emphasizing in our time—the availability of Christ for today. He is alive and moving and living among us. We do not worship a dead Christ, one that can be kept in a tomb. He escapes every prison house.

Yes, our faith is not a hitching post which ties him down, which anchors him in a tomb, which buries him in a book. It is a guidepost declaring the living reality of our Lord, offering his Presence to walk through life's joys and sorrows with us. Jesus does not wave to us from the past; he beckons to us from the future. He is alive forevermore. The greatest assurance we have of life after death rests in Jesus' word when he said, "Because I live, you shall live also."

Christianity is not a hitching post which ties us to the ashes and dust of this world but rather a guidepost pointing the way and bringing us assurance of our eternal home. Jesus does not wave to us from the past but beckons to us from the future—*this is our faith!*

Hymns: "I Know that My Redeemer Lives"
"Savior, Like a Shepherd Lead Us"

Scripture: Matthew 28:16-20

PRAYER

Eternal God, who has loved us into life and who loves us through life into life eternal, once again we pause seeking your ear and listening for your voice.

We are continually overwhelmed at your majesty and greatness and yet humbled in gratitude for your personal concern in our lives. Nothing escapes your notice or is foreign to your understanding. You always listen, as a parent to a child, to our every prayer. Every detail of our lives is of interest to you. What would we do, O God, without your love, without your courage, without your strength, without your comfort?

Steady those who are faced with uncertainty. Awaken those who find life drab and colorless. Give us courage to stand for truth, to say no when it is so easy to say yes, to be true to the highest we know. Help us walk as your children. In Christ's name we pray. AMEN.

FACING LIFE'S BROKEN DREAMS

We all have our dreams broken, our plans changed, our lives altered. What we do with our broken dreams, what we do in spite of them, and even because of them, determines our future and value to both God and others.

Some forget broken dreams momentarily through drug and drink. And you can for a time escape the anguish of a broken dream. You can live in another world, a world of make-believe. But the tragedy of this way of escape is that you soon return to your prison cell, behind bars which become stronger and iron doors more securely locked. This way of escape only intensifies disappointment and offers no solution.

Some respond to a broken dream by resentment and self-pity. This way is to rebel and protest. Why did this have to happen to me? There is no justice in it. What have I done to deserve this? But life closes in around the person who drowns in self-pity and who gives in to the poison of resentment.

And then some respond with a stoical gritting of the teeth, an "I can take it" attitude. They resolve to go grimly through with it. No meaning is seen in the disappointment, only a determination to stand fast and dare it to hurt or encroach further.

But there is another way. It is to accept the disappointment and try through God's help to use it for good. It is to pick up the broken pieces and fit them into a mosaic. It is to trust in the words of Paul when he said, "All things work together for good to them that love God" (Romans 8:28). It is to accept your limitation, sorrow, illness, misfortune, and ask that God help you use it for some good. It is a faith which says that there is a merciful God whose plans are not completed here, who offers us strength to withstand life's disappointments, and who helps us to triumph over them.

Such was the way in which Handel met his broken dream. At Christmastime we always turn our thoughts to the greatest musical composition of that blessed season—Handel's *Messiah*. It speaks to us of the love of God, his mercy, and his redeeming grace. Yet, when Handel wrote it, he had already lost his health, his money, and his friends. His creditors hounded him every day, threatening to throw him into prison. His right side was almost completely paralyzed. Yet, this man took his limitations and gloriously set them to music, unforgettable music about the love of God.

Turning from music to art, here is Millet and his lovely "Angelus". You recall how it pictures the peasants who at sunset paused to pray while the church bells rang. We are told that when Millet painted that picture, the roof of his life was full of holes. His health was poor. There was only a two-day supply of fuel. His mother was dying and he didn't have the money to go to her. So discouraged was he that he contemplated suicide, but instead he gave the world his greatest picture, the "Angelus."

Whatever may be your imitation, your broken dream, your disappointment, your sorrow, dedicate it to God and ask God to help you work with it, even in spite of it, that you may know that "all things work together for good to them that love God."

Hymns: "O God, Our Help in Ages Past"
"I Love Thy Kingdom, Lord"

Scripture: Luke 12:22-32

PRAYER

O God, we do not know what the day or the hour will bring forth but only at this moment you make an instant claim on our lives. Grant that we may open the door of our hearts so that your Spirit may enter in.

Forbid that we should deny or delay that claim. From you we came, and to you our spirits will return; without you we are restless until we find our rest in you. Help us to know that life's most important quest is in finding you and being found by you.

Comfort us this day with the fact that our problems cannot be adequately met without your strength and your wisdom. May we purge from our lives all that would shut out your power and your presence. Help us to be hard on ourselves in disciplining our wayward desires. Grant that we may want to fashion our wills according to your way.

Where there is family disorder, bring peace.
Where there are temptations, bring strength.

Where there are sorrowful hearts, bring comfort.
Where there is lingering illness, bring healing.
Where there are bitter spirits, bring love.
Where there is crippling fear, bring hope.
Where there is disturbing doubt, bring faith.

Remind us once again that you do not leave us comfortless or powerless, but you are always standing by, through Jesus Christ. Amen.

SUCH AS I HAVE, I GIVE

In the third chapter of Acts we find Peter and John going up to the temple to pray. It was three o'clock in the afternoon, and by the gate lay a lame man in his accustomed place, asking for help.

When he spoke to them, Peter said: "Look at us." And the lame man fixed his attention upon them, expecting to receive something from them. But Peter said, "I have no silver or gold, but what I have I give you; in the name of Jesus Christ of Nazareth stand up and walk" (verse 6).

Now Peter is here expressing what every disciple in a measure can declare. Such as we all have, we can give. As someone has put it, "The moneyless can show mercy; the poorest can give to the poor sympathy and consideration." In other words, all of us have possessions which we can share.

The greatest gifts we possess are those things which when given away do not diminish, but increase in quantity as well as quality. Material gifts are always acceptable, but the real value of a gift is in what it represents.

If we are given something, its genuine significance lies in the thought or motive behind it. A child's wild daisies given out of deep love mean more than an expensive orchid given with no thought of affection. A gift is valued by the heart that gives it.

Love and kindness are a possession worth sharing. There are millions of people the world over and hundreds around us starving, not for bread, but for the milk of human kindness. There are bruised spirits, suffering from hastily spoken words and harsh deeds, who long for sympathy that comes from a heart filled with love.

Hymns: "Rise Up, O Men of God"
"O Master, Let Me Walk with Thee"

Scripture: Acts 3:1-10

PRAYER

Eternal God, you have made us and you do not forsake us. In you we live and move and have our being. In you there is no

27

darkness, and from you we find light for life's journey. Open our hearts and minds to you this day.

We thank you for the world you have prepared for us as our dwelling place. We thank you for rising and setting suns, seedtime and harvest, summer and winter. We thank you for the great open spaces—the plains with all their expanse and breath-taking beauty. We are grateful for the majesty of the mountains and the mighty roar of the sea. We are filled with wonder before the starry sky and the constellations on high. In it all we see your hand as Creator and source of all beauty. Indeed the heavens declare your glory and the firmament shows your handiwork.

But beyond the creation of your hands we are filled with awe before you as we know you in Christ. We are overwhelmed with your love as expressed in the Cross; such suffering love commands our love in return.

We would this day express to you our devotion and loyalty. With reverent hearts and dedicated minds we give ourselves to you. We want to follow your way, for we know it is the only way which leads to peace and joy. Help us to be strong when we are tempted to do evil. Help us to be loving when it is easy to hate. Make us forgiving as you forgive us. Give us strength to withstand illness, and give us courage in the face of danger.

And in the light of Christ's love, help us to find the way. Amen.

LIFE BEGINS AT EASTER

For many people life is not worth living. The cares of yesterday added with those of today and in anticipation of those of tomorrow are too much to bear. But over against such despair we come to Easter looking for something which will give us new hope and a new lease on life.

We come not merely because we want to see and be seen, but because deep down we seek for renewed hope about life and about life eternal. We come in the hope that life will reach new heights and will take on deeper significance and clearer meanings.

Certainly we feel that unless there is more to life than we sometimes suspect there is, then indeed it is not worth living. Unless the way to which Jesus pointed is true, there is little hope for any of us. Time and time again we come to an impasse which confronts us with the fact that we cannot carry on in our own strength.

The strains of daily living, the misunderstandings with others in our lives, burdens that grief places upon us, the temptations that easily beset us—these weigh heavily upon us and break our backs unless we can turn to "everlasting arms" which can uphold us.

So, on Easter we come reminding ourselves that Jesus is the one who takes the person who doesn't want to live and makes that person fall in love with life again. Jesus says, "I came that they may have life, and have it abundantly" (John 10:10), and again "Because I live, you will live also" (John 14:19).

We can see this new life at work in those early disciples. After the crucifixion they scattered in despair. They did not know which way to turn, for the light of their life had gone out. Peter was brokenhearted over his denial, and the others were weighted down for having run away. But after that first Easter morning a new power came into their lives, for they knew their Lord had risen and was with them always.

Today this same spirit is here touching our lives and putting new life into them. He is one who turns our sorrow into abiding joy; fear into courage; routine and dullness into thrilling adventure. He can take a person without a purpose and give that person a reason for living. He takes those of us who do not want to live and makes us fall in love with life again.

Indeed! Life *begins* at Easter!

Hymns: "O for a Thousand Tongues to Sing"
"Christ the Lord Is Risen Today"

Scripture: Luke 16:9-20

PRAYER

O eternal God, you who have proven your love for humanity by sending your Son Jesus Christ, our Lord, to lighten our darkness and to illumine our pathway, we praise you for this your gift.

We remember his passion and sacrifice for sinful humanity; we remember his death and resurrection, which have changed the course of history, and which offer eternal life to all who believe on his name.

We bow before you today, conscious of our sins and shortcomings. We have done those things which we ought not to have done and left undone those things which we ought to have done. O God, have mercy upon us.

Forgive us when our thoughts have wandered far from you; when harsh words have been hastily spoken; and when unkind deeds have been thoughtlessly committed.

Open our minds and hearts to your companionship. Free us from our preoccupation with the cares of this world, that we may hear your still small voice. Breathe into our discordant lives a portion of your peace. Reassure us of your love as we face the uncertainties of tomorrow. Undergird us with your strength. Lighten our pathway with the light of truth as we grope through the darkness of difficult decisions. Inspire us with your presence and let us know that we love and labor and laugh, not alone but with you.

Send us out with your truth and the power to do your will, through Jesus Christ our Lord. AMEN.

LOVE, A LANGUAGE EVERYONE UNDERSTANDS

God knew that love is a language everyone understands, so God sent Jesus into the world. In Jesus Christ we see the incarnation of love. He appeals to people of all ages, of all races, of all clans—because they see in him love.

There is no word in any language today that deserves more attention than this little four-letter word—L O V E. The extent of its application into today's world determines the future of humankind. Basic in every marriage bond, essential in all lasting friendships, necessary in all relationships—this word holds the key to that brave new world of which we dream and toward which we strive.

It was because of this that Paul said, "And now faith, hope, and love abide, these three; and the greatest of these is love" (I Corinthians 13:13).

Later it tells us to pursue love. This is the supreme virtue. Paul was right. Life's greatest virtue is love. And Jesus Christ is the incarnation of love, the highest expression of it we know, and he commanded his disciples that they should love one another. He insisted that his followers be known by their love for him and for one another. Jesus came not to lay down a set of rules for human behavior but to manifest a spirit, a new way of life. Without this spirit of love, life is incomplete, imperfect, and defective.

Let us look at this love which completes life and crowns it.

In the first place, *knowledge without love leads to nothing*. Paul says, "If I have prophetic powers, and understand all mysteries and all knowledge, and if I have all faith, so as to remove mountains, but do not have love, I am nothing" (I Corinthians 13:2). He is telling us that knowledge, learning, and scientific progress avail for nothing unless at the heart there is good will.

How true his words are today! We have explored the mysteries of life. We have fashioned in laboratories that which can lengthen life. We have conquered the air with planes and the sea with ships. We have shortened space and lengthened time with our labor-saving devices. Our world has been squeezed into a neighborhood through the machine.

Yet, what has happened? In our laboratory where vaccines have been produced to lengthen lives, we have also produced gases which would shorten them. Our planes have conquered the air and have borne medicine and food for people in need, but they can still threaten the existence of millions. Ships which connected continents and brought them closer together have been used in our time to push them farther apart.

Paul says that it is not enough to gain wisdom. Wisdom must be directed by a loving will.

In the second place, *love is a contribution everyone can make*. We should never be tempted to underestimate the importance of that which we can add to the enrichment of life, however small it may seem to us. One bucketful of water will not quench a raging fire, but the principle is right and many bucketfuls will do it.

Our life is placed in a system of relations, and into that web we each can pour our contribution of love and good will. It is life dropping a pebble into a still pool. No section of that pool is undisturbed by the movement.

Love is a contribution all can make. We can love one another wherever we are. We can let go from our lives the light of love lighted by the central sun, Jesus Christ, from whose energy we draw our light. We can refuse to hate when others have abused us. We can enlarge our circle of love by including people we do not like. We can love those of other races and offer them opportunities equal to our own.

Finally, *the future belongs to love*. It belongs to love because it is a language everyone can understand and that everyone can speak. The future belongs to love because it enriches the one who gives it as well as the one who receives it. But even more, the future belongs to love because it belongs to God, and God is love. All hatred, falsehood, fear, cruelty, enmity, and bitterness are doomed by love. The resurrection of Christ is the symbol telling us that victory belongs to love, that evil and hatred cannot hold sway over it.

Hymns: "O Love That Wilt Not Let Me Go"
            "Blest Be the Tie That Binds"

Scripture: I Corinthians 13

Prayer

Eternal God, whose days are without end and whose mercies cannot be numbered, we give you our humble and hearty thanks for the world you have prepared and furnished for our dwelling place. We thank you for rising and setting suns, for seedtime and harvests, summer and winter, and for daily comforts which minister to our lives. Help us to be grateful for the many ways in which you bless us. Move us to express our thanks to you for life and for the days of our years.

But above all, O God, we thank you for yourself and for the wonder and majesty of your love—a love that will not let us go—a love that touches our lives even when we are unaware of it—a love that shames us in our unworthiness and yet moves us to nobler living—a love always ready to receive us when we wander from your house.

Speak to our needs this day, we pray.

Where there is sorrow, bring comfort.

Where there is fear, give assurance.

Where there is loneliness, offer companionship.

Where there is illness, rest your healing hand.

Where there is guilt, offer forgiveness.

Where there is discouragement, bring hope.

Lift us, gracious God, out of ourselves as we gaze upon your matchless beauty and send us forth strengthened by your spirit, through Christ our Lord. Amen.

BEHIND WAS PRIVATE SOLITUDE

In Mark 1:35 we have these words: "He . . . went out to a deserted place, and there he prayed." It was in this lonely place we find the secret of Jesus' power and the renewal of that power.

Behind his whole public ministry, when great crowds were gathered around him, when matchless words came forth from his lips, when men and women were given new hope in life—behind it all was this private solitude. The lonely place of prayer. Here was the hidden spring of authority. Out of this lonely place came that power which amazed all who heard him.

For Jesus it was not a time out for prayer. It was rather a time for renewal of life, for fresh adjustment to the will of God. It was a time for replenishment of the power of God. Here new energies flowed into his life. Here the weariness which had overtaken him gave way to renewed strength. Indeed, rather than being a time out for prayer, it was the most important time that he spent. All that he did had its reference to this lonely place. In fact, without these moments his public ministry would have been in vain.

And for us who follow him the same is true. If we would find the purpose for life, the meaning to existence, the road to travel, we cannot neglect prayer. If we are to find solace for sorrow, strength for weakness, and courage for fear, then prayer cannot be neglected.

It is impossible to be adequately religious apart from prayer—for religion is really living with God. And as our earthly friendships depend on frequent intercommunication—so with our friendship with God.

For Jesus, going out to a lonely place and praying was not a passive act, but the highest activity of mind and spirit. To be sure, he was not as active as when he was healing those crowded around him. But true activity is not measured by noise or motion.

Someone passed a young forest of trees which had been planted years ago. It was a lovely scene. The pines were tall and straight and underneath a soft bed of needles. Along the highway was this sign: "Quiet, Trees at Work." Nothing seemed to be happening, but these trees were busy at work, quietly, silently opening themselves to the unseen forces of their environment.

So this for Jesus was the secret of his life and power—opening his soul to the unseen forces of his environment—God.

It can be for you and me the secret of our lives. It is in these lonely places where we meet God that life finds its true dimension of height.

But these lonely places do not just happen. They are made. Jesus never happened to find himself alone. He had to go out and find a place and a time. Jesus set the example for us in telling us to get alone, away from "prying or approving eyes" to a place we make a sanctuary. To have an accustomed place adds something to the value of our prayer life. Being creatures of habit, we associate our experiences with the surroundings we are in. The setting gives a remembrance that helps.

Not only a place but a time. This is not easy. But unless we have a set time during the day when we are alone with God, the danger is that we will fail to pray. Our lives are ordered on schedules. We go to work at a certain time. We eat at a fixed hour. We go to bed around the same time every night. We live by the clock. And unless in this crowded schedule we make definite room for prayer, we may find our day filled with activities that have encroached on time that belongs to God. We need to "take time to be holy." This does not mean that we shall spend long hours in meditation and prayer, for many of us would frankly feel cramped to do so. We need not pray by the clock to the extent of any certain period. But we should have a period of the day which is unhurried and without strain.

This time for prayer in our high-pressured life may of necessity vary with each person. Many have found the early morning to be most fruitful. Our minds are fresh; our day lies before us unlived; our bodies are rested.

Many saints have made use of very early hours for such meditation; some even have risen at four in the morning. For most of us this is not practical, but we can turn our waking thoughts to God and dedicate the day's work and activity to the Creator.

Hymns: "Sweet Hour of Prayer"
    "Be Still, My Soul"

Scripture: Mark 1:32-45

O God eternal, in the midst of the rush and hurry of life we pause in your presence to get our bearings. In you we find our way in life and through you our strength for life. Change and decay all around we may see, but you are changeless.

Here in this place today drive out, we pray, all fear of what the future may bring. Take from us the strain and stress and let our ordered lives confess the beauty of your peace. Prepare us in body, mind, and soul for life's unexpectedness. Set our feet upon foundations whose builder and maker is God. Help us to know that all things work together for good to them that love you. Grant that we may discover how the sorrows and pains of life can be used for good. Bind up our worries and heartaches with your tender love and touch. Speak to us words of comfort and courage.

Send us forth today strengthened by your Spirit. Through him who is always standing by, the same Jesus Christ our Lord. AMEN.

CUPS OF COLD WATER

In the forty-second verse of the tenth chapter of Matthew we have these words: "Whoever gives even a cup of cold water to one of these little ones in the name of a disciple—truly I tell you, none of these will lose their reward."

Here Jesus is stressing the divine evaluation of the elementary kindly service. Now anyone who has been to the Holy Land in the hot season of the year can see with deeper insight what Jesus was talking about in "a cup of cold water." In this dry and thirsty land this act of kindness has great meaning.

I recall traveling with a group one day from Amman, in Jordan, to Petra, some 180 miles south, with only a bottle of warm water to quench our thirst. Having been delayed for four hours because of road repairs, we spent from seven o'clock in the morning until twelve midnight on the trip, and the only water available was a little warm water from a bottle. Indeed, we knew what Jesus meant by this figure of speech.

But here he was using it as a symbol, and this symbol was for kindness. It is meeting life at a point of need. Kindness makes our Christian life more convincing. Christianity cannot, like some religions, be undisturbed in the presence of physical need.

To be sure, life at times may seem a barren and parched affair with no cups of water. When we look at the misery and heartache in our world today, when we see the conflict that rages between nations, we think of the world as a cold, cruel place. But having said that, let us not forget that there is kindness too. Where there are forces which would destroy, there are also forces that would heal. Where there are ruthless individuals, there are also charitable people. Though there are those who push others down, there are also those who lift them up.

Along the journey of life we see this cup of cold water given in unexpected places. I saw this happen in the Middle East, that part of the world which is predominantly Moslem in religion.

We had been riding some four or five hours over a dry and dusty highway. Over our mouths were damp handkerchiefs, and, in fact, most of the time we had to breathe through a handkerchief. We had little water in the car.

As we rounded a curve we saw a man who was tending sheep running toward the highway. Our driver stopped, for he understood the signal of this shepherd. As he got out of the car, he took a bottle of water with him and gave the man a drink. Indeed, it was a cup of cold water.

In the tenth verse of the twelfth chapter of Romans Paul writes: "Love one another with mutual affection; outdo one another in showing honor." Here Paul is giving emphasis to the fact that there is no greater need in the world today than kindness and thoughtfulness extended to one another. To be sure the world starves in some quarters for food, but far greater than this need is that of love and kindness. A kind word, a thoughtful deed, a genuine appreciation, a friendly handclasp, a token of encouragement—such lifts in unexpected places and from unexpected sources have often changed the course of a person's life.

Kindness is really a positive thing. It costs so little to mean much. We must think about it and cultivate it. Let's try to go out of our way to be kind to others. Let us say with William Penn, "I expect to pass through this life but once. If therefore, there be any kindness I can show, or any good thing I can do to any fellow being, let me do it now, and not defer or neglect it, as I shall not pass this way again."

Hymns: "They'll Know We Are Christians"
"Let There Be Peace on Earth"

Scripture: Matthew 10:39-42

PRAYER

O God, in whose love we learn the meaning and through whose strength we bear the burden and cross of life, give us the courage to stand for truth and righteousness even if it requires cost to ourselves. Grant that people may know what it means to love when they look at our lives, that they may understand the meaning of Jesus' command to return good for evil, to do good to all. Help us so to love that others might see some reflection of your unending love for all people.

Grant that by our lives we may bear witness to our faith that anyone who trusts in Christ becomes a new creature. Give to us, we pray, the consciousness of your Holy Spirit, which guides us and empowers us and strengthens us. Send us forth to live at our best. AMEN.

LIFE'S HEALING POWER

Immediately after Jesus was baptized by John, he went into the desert to remain for forty days and there be tempted and tested. Mark says Jesus "was in the company of wild beasts; and the angels ministered to him."

Mark alone mentions the wild beasts, and for him they serve either to intensify the loneliness of the wilderness or to typify the strong, merciless character of the forces of evil.

The angels may very well symbolize the forces of righteousness and purity ever present in the arena of the soul's struggle. They may represent to us today life's healing powers at work in God's world. Certainly when we reflect upon life's uncertainties and evils, we can see certain forces that minister to our needs.

Healing powers are at our disposal in the physical world. Let us look at this force which we may call life's healing power at work in the realm of plant life. Look at trees where limbs have been severed, and soon we will discover a protective covering that heals the wounds of that tree.

Perhaps in animal life the healing powers of life are more evident to us, for it is where we live. Broken fingers to broken backs are healed. When we get a wound on our bodies, immediately there are forces within the body which start their healing functions. It is amazing to witness this power at work.

A physician who has performed hundreds of autopsies claims that many human ills are cured before the victims even know they had the affliction. Proof was found that the healing forces had quietly done their work without being specially called in.

Every decade witnesses new medical discoveries and new drugs which help prolong life. Yet, after doctors and nurses have done all they can, they must in the final analysis rely on life's healing powers to mend their patients.

The father of French surgery in the sixteenth century, Ambroise Paré, had these words inscribed over the door of a hospital in Paris: "I dress the wound; God heals it."

There is another area of life no less real and in reality more important than the physical world, and that is this power at work in the spiritual realm. It is at work when a loved one dies. How unbearable seem the hours! Life seems to hold no meaning for the future. But gradually and surely this healing power helps us withstand and carry on. It heals our inner wounds. When we are afraid, this power will give us courage. When we are lonely, this power gives comfort. When our spirits sin and wander into a far country, this power is still at work to heal our wounds. The Prodigal's return was this power at work. Sometimes we call it conscience, but in reality it is God at work.

Now this power at work in the world of nature—in plant life, in animal life, social progress, and spiritual life—is one and the same power. It is God at work in the world. It is a personal power that touches us where we live. It is a power that would save us in all areas of life.

Hymns: "O Master, Let Me Walk with Thee"
        "My Faith Looks Up to Thee"

Scripture: Mark 1:1-13

Prayer

Eternal God, in whom we live and move and have our being, we give you our gratitude for life's healing powers. We know that, as you have made us, it is within your power to restore life when it is in need of repair.

We are thankful for all your servants who do your bidding in ministering to our broken bodies. We are grateful for the tender concern, the skilled hands, and the trained minds of nurses who give of themselves in dedicated service. We thank you for doctors whose long years of study bring a healing ministry to those in distress. We are grateful for the generosity of many who have given of their substance that institutions of healing may bring aid to the sick in mind and body. We thank you for friends and loved ones who watch beside beds of pain, and for all who offer prayers to you for recovery. In their ministries we feel something of your concern for our lives, and we are grateful. Amen.

GETTING ALONG WITH PEOPLE

One of the most important things we have to learn is to get along with people. Now, at this stage of our lives, we should have long ago learned this art, but it seems we need to learn it again and again. We are social beings and on every hand relate ourselves to others. Unless we learn to live peaceably with all kinds of people life will be bitter and hard.

Now, being able to get along does not mean necessarily that one is agreeable to everything that happens. Not at all. There is a way to disagree without being disagreeable, to stand for principle without stirring up a cyclone, to have convictions without being obnoxious. To be sure, there may come a time or situation in which a person will break step with others and in so doing gain their disapproval and even their enmity.

But we must cultivate the art of relating ourselves happily to other people without sacrificing principle and conviction. Let us consider some practical suggestions as we seek to cultivate this art.

In the first place, *we should learn to differ without getting angry.* This is one of the hardest things we have to do. There are people who simply cannot tolerate any disagreement. They take such as a personal attack, which, of course, makes it hard for them to get along with others. The chances are that such people are unsure of themselves, which makes them hold fast to their own notions lest they lose stature.

Learning to differ without being disagreeable is to recognize that no one has all the answers or the whole truth. It is to be teachable.

After William E. Gladstone died, the widow of the great statesman discovered in his private papers a long list of names which bore the title, "Those who have disagreed with me." Below were penned these words in Gladstone's handwriting: "Good for me to remember what notable people have differed with me."

Second, *the person who gets along is one who is sincerely interested in what is happening to others.* Rather than bore others with the details of their own operations, such people inquire with real interest into the details of others' problems.

I know a lady who has had few advantages in life. She lives in a small community and is married to a man whose income is very modest. She has never been to college, but many people who have go to her for advice. They like to be around her because of her genuine concern in what is happening to them.

This interest in other people goes deeper than surface concern or an interest based on a selfish motive. It is based on a deep respect for personality. It sees people as ends, of great value within themselves, and never as means to some selfish, personal end.

A third suggestion is: *Take your share of the load.* There are some people who are always ready to lead but never to follow. They want to be forever in the limelight, and unless they are, they will not play the game. They are willing to give but not to take orders. Longfellow once said, "The talent of success is nothing more than doing what you can well, and doing whatever you do without any thought of fame." Another has well said that there is no telling the amount of good one person can do if he is not too interested in who gets the credit.

Hymns: "Come Thou Fount of Every Blessing"
"Where Cross the Crowded Ways of Life"

Scripture: I John 3:1-11

PRAYER

O God from whose hands come life's gifts and through whose servants we are blessed, grant that we may ever be aware of those who make life fuller for us. Forbid that we should accept their services without gratitude or that we should ever take them for granted. For countless thousands who daily minister to our needs we give thanks.

For those who paint our houses and clean our walls, may their ladders hold firm and their scaffolds be steady.

For those who serve food every day, grant them strength for long hours of toil and patience in handling details.

For the postal worker who brings us news on bad and good days, go with that person on the daily round.

For the police officers keeping guard over our community, give them a sense of dignity in their work and through the long night-watches a consciousness of your abiding presence.

For the doctors, grant unusual strength and health as they go about answering our calls of distress.

Through these and all your servants our lives are made richer, and we give you our gratitude for their ministries. AMEN.

NOW IS THE TIME

One of the greatest Christian leaders of the early church, Augustine, once said, "Man lives by the tradition of the past, in the hope of the future, but makes his decisions in the present." No truer statement has ever been made concerning our lives, and it is especially appropriate in this hour of the world's history.

We cannot possibly separate ourselves from the past, the future, or the present. The life we live today is related to that of yesterday and determines that of tomorrow.

Let us look at the phrase "lives by the tradition of the past." We certainly cannot separate ourselves from that which has gone before. To a great extent we are products of the past not only in biological inheritance but also in social inheritance. We are but the lengthened shadows of our forebears. We benefit by the experience of others through the ages, and foolish is the one who refuses to listen to what history can teach.

But tradition becomes a millstone when we not only accept it as a background but refuse to move out from it into the present and future. There are those who are living today on the religious experience of their forebears. They have not found God for themselves, but all these years have been dependent upon mother's, father's, or grandmother's religious experience. To depend upon another's religious experience is no more satisfying than to depend upon the food another eats. The past is a hindrance when it is continually referred to as a substitute for the present. You have undoubtedly been to a city or village which seemed to be living only in the past, one which reveled in its tradition and was existing only in the memory of it.

It is not enough to "live in the tradition of the past"; we must live "in the hope of the future." Augustine means by this that we must always have our eyes pointed to the future. We, to be sure, cannot live in the present unless we have our eyes pointed to the future. In the future there is always hope. Even when hope has faded from this earthly realm, there is hope of the future grounded in a good and kind God.

But to live in the tradition of the past and in the hope of the future is not enough, for as Augustine said, we make our decisions in the present. This is the whole crux of the matter. Decisions must be made now. There are too many who are looking backward at those made in the past or to the future to those that will be made then. Now is the time!

In Joshua 24:15 we find these words: "Choose this day whom you will serve." This note of urgency needs to be struck today. Now is the time! Choose this day whom you will serve.

In this verse we can see how Joshua was challenging his people with a loyalty to Jehovah, their God. He was making the matter urgent. Choose this day, he was saying. It is not enough to look backward to the day your parents were loyal to God or even when you first made your covenant with God. Nor is it enough to look to tomorrow for your fidelity to God; but, rather, now is the time.

Now is the time for us to decide what we shall do with Jesus the Christ. We see him standing there at the head of the column of humanity. Shall we dare to follow him? There are many today with good intentions who say, "Maybe tomorrow I will decide." They are like Augustine who before his conversion prayed, "Give me purity, O Lord, but not just now." But time ticks on and no one knows what the morrow holds in store. There are great decisions every human soul should make. We dare not put them off until tomorrow. One decision all must make: Will we or will we not accept Christ?

In an old legend we find the story of a man walking through an enchanted forest. Suddenly he came upon a sundial and saw on it these words, "It is later than you think." So it is. We must be in haste. Now is the time for us to have dealings with God and to start life afresh—resolve to live a finer, cleaner, nobler life. Yes, "Man lives by the tradition of the past, in the hope of the future, but makes his decisions in the present." "Choose this day whom you will serve." *Now is the time!*

Hymns: "O Jesus, Thou Art Standing"
          "Only Trust Him"

Scripture: Joshua 24:14-18

Prayer

Eternal God, in whom we live and move and have our being, with thankful hearts we praise your holy name. This is your world, and we are your children living in your house. But we bow our heads in shame because we have not lived as kindred one with another. Our selfishness and pride have separated us; our prejudice has divided us. We have not loved one another as you have willed that we should. Forgive us.

We come, too, confessing our sin in thinking too highly of ourselves. We know that we are weak and frail beings in need of a Redeemer and a Savior who can lift us out of our sordid selves. So we come to you today in need of the Christ who is the Savior of the world and who alone can save us from sin. Take us this day and make us more worthy servants, through Jesus Christ. Amen.

GOD IS ABLE

One of the great problems that face us today is despair. When we come upon some situation which seems too much for us the real temptation is to lose heart. When we are confronted with obstacles which seem insurmountable, we too often retreat, acknowledging defeat. When we look at what ought to be done and then why it seems impossible to do it, we throw up our hands and say, "Not now!"

But most of the time when we feel defeated and overcome with despair, we forget that there are resources other than our own, that God is able to see us through.

It is interesting to note that there is a recurring theme in our Bible which says: God is able. In Jude 24 the writer is apparently speaking to those who face temptations when he writes: "Now to him who is able to keep you from falling." Paul puts it this way in Romans 14:4: "The Lord is able to make them stand."

When we are tempted to confine God within the boundaries of our own inadequate calculations and feel that God is limited within our cramping expectations, let us listen to these words from Ephesians 3:20: "Now to him who by the power at work within us is able to accomplish abundantly far more than all we can ask or imagine."

And in II Corinthians 9:8 Paul continues to affirm the power of God when he writes: "God is able to provide you with every good blessing in abundance, so that by always having enough of everything, you may share abundantly in every good work."

Indeed, God is able. God is alive and active in our affairs. God is still in command of the world. He possesses the forces which can change our hearts, and this change can alter the tides of time. For God is able, not only on the world scene but also in our personal lives. When we face despair, when we meet obstacles, to be sure we must take into account the physical resources at hand. It is only right that we explore to the fullest the brains given us and the talents available. But after that, let's not rule out God.

Maybe some of you feel that your life is a failure. You are in despair. Sin has made you sick. You no longer gain joy out of living. Life has no meaning. You are ready to throw in the towel.

Or perhaps some of you feel that life has crowded you into a corner and you see no way out—only a dead-end street. Tragedy has come your way. It may be through broken health. It may be financial distress. It may be an aching sorrow. It may be a handicap of physical limitation.

Well, here is hope for you. Our God "is able to provide you with every blessing." God is able to take what seems to be a hopeless, helpless person and make that person whole again. God can take a person who does not want to live and make that person fall in love with life again.

Paul, the great apostle, a man of dynamic action and creative ability, once said, "We were so utterly, unbearably crushed that we despaired of life itself" (II Corinthians 1:8); and yet he said, "God is able to make them stand," and in that faith he became the world's greatest missionary.

There is no greater need in our time than that of counting on God. To be sure, God expects us to use to the fullest all the gifts and powers with which we are endowed, to be as wise as our wisdom will let us be; but God also expects us to leave some things to him, to live by faith.

Hymns: "All Hail the Power of Jesus' Name"
        "Faith of Our Fathers"

Scripture: Ephesians 3

PRAYER

O God, again we come into your presence marveling at your care for our lives, overwhelmed at your goodness to us. Showered upon us from all sides are manifestations of your love, O God:

Were it not for your love, life would be barren.

Were it not for moments of prayer, we would stumble and not get up.

Were it not for your goodness, our lives would perish.

Were it not for your mercy, our sins would destroy us.

Were it not for your abiding presence, we would grope in the darkness.

Were it not for you, O God, life would be too much for us. But with you we live our days in confidence and face the unexpected in trust. O God:

With you, life's cares cannot stagger us.

With you, life's sorrows mellow our spirits and deepen our understanding.

With you, life's disappointments become new opportunities.

With you, life's dangers are faced with courage.

With you, life's mysteries hold no fear.

With you, life's days are filled to overflowing with joy. In Christ's name, we pray. Amen.

GOD NEVER LETS US ALONE

Sometimes in a world like our own it is easy for us to feel that God lets us alone. When so much that is tragic faces us today, it is easy to get the idea that God has forsaken us. Some doubts express themselves in questions like these: "What is God doing now?" "Oh, if I knew where to find God! I know what I need, but where can I find God?" "God doesn't seem real to me."

But we find an answer to these inquiries about God forsaking us in words that assure us that God never lets us alone. In Revelation 3:20 we find these words: "Listen! I am standing at the door knocking; if you hear my voice and open the door, I will come in to you and eat with you, and you with me."

These words express an eternal truth that the God and Father of our Lord Jesus Christ is one who never lets us alone. He continually haunts us with his presence. When we think we are done with God, again and again God comes back to us.

"Listen! I am standing at the door knocking." God is always near us. Ever about our lives he hovers. Continually he is knocking at the door of our hearts. In numerous ways God is trying to be heard, is asking for admittance, is wanting to come in.

"If you hear my voice . . ." This suggests to us that the sound of God's approach can be heard, that we have been given ears that can listen to God's knocking. God's ways are numerous. God is not limited to one approach to our hearts. Different as we are in tastes and talents, so are God's different means of entrance into our lives.

Let us consider the many ways in which the voice of God can be heard. A man once confessed that God became most real to him while he was visiting a slum area of a large city. He said the contrast between the ugliness and sorrow found there and the purity and beauty of what God must be like struck him. God in such unlovely conditions became a voice knocking at the door of his heart.

So one way in which the Eternal knocks at the doors of our hearts is through suffering, trouble, and heartache. Somehow we are so conditioned by tragedy that God's voice is heard.

Others of us see God in that which is beautiful; we hear the voice of God through loveliness. It may be in the splash of color that strikes our eyes at the close of day when we look at the sunset. It may be in listening to lovely music that speaks of eternal values. It may be in the face of a person whose lines and sense of poise remind us of a Presence. God makes beauty in the world to knock at our hearts. So when we are in the presence of such, let us listen, for at that moment God is asking entrance into our lives.

Again in the midst of danger which is met bravely by some courageous soul, in the midst of heavy odds faced by indomitable will, at these moments God is suggesting himself to us.

Then, too, in times of stillness and quietness, the presence of God in Christ comes to us. It may be in the still of the night as it was for Samuel, or in the light of day when we are quiet, that God knocks. God has said, "Be still, and know that I am God" (Psalm 46:10). How afraid we are of stillness and quietness! We need to be still and reflect on life and what it is all about. But we are too busy going somewhere or meeting with others.

It is not enough just to hear and then fail to open the door. But we must respond to what we hear; we must invite God in as a guest. This power of responding has been given to us. God does not force us to open the door, but has left the power of acceptance to us. To be sure, God has made us, and we will be restless until we open the door, but God does not open the door for us.

"I will come in to you and eat with you, and you with me." When we hand God the key, God will come in as a guest and dine with us. God will become for us a companion, a friend, a counselor, a power. God's presence will show through the light of our eyes. It will reveal itself in our dealing with people. It will make itself felt as we face unbearable burdens. It will give us confidence as we face an uncertain future. It will send us down the days of our years singing. When God comes in as our guest cynicism will disappear. Love and joy will fill our days.

Hymns: "How Firm a Foundation"
"My Hope Is Built on Nothing Less"

Scripture: Luke 21:25-33

PRAYER

Once again, O God, we pause to be still and know that you are God. You have been our dwelling place in all generations. Before the mountains were brought forth or ever you had formed the earth, even from everlasting to everlasting, you are God. In the midst of a changing and uncertain world we turn to you, knowing that you never change. Help us to hold this thought in our minds and in our hearts and to be not afraid.

Steady us as we make decisions.

Strengthen us as we face complexities.

Lure us with goodness as we are tempted to do evil.

Fasten our eyes upon the beautiful when we are faced with the sordid.

Fix our minds upon high and noble thoughts that our lives may be fashioned into your likeness.

Grant that we may look at life not through the eyes of prejudice but through the eyes of love and reason.

Give us brave hearts and a strong will so that whatever life brings to us we may use it for good, through Jesus Christ our Lord, in whose name we pray. Amen.

FAITH THAT NEEDS NO EXPLANATION

"I know the one in whom I have put my trust, and I am sure that he is able to guard until that day what I have entrusted to him" (II Timothy 1:12). This is how Paul expressed his faith to his young friend Timothy. He wrote this notwithstanding the fact that his life since becoming a Christian had been fraught with great hardship. Almost from the first moment that he accepted Christ hardships were his. His Christian life started in flight as he escaped the angry mob in Damascus by being lowered in a basket through a hole in the city wall. In spite of all his sufferings and thwarted dreams he forged a faith in God that did not ask for explanation in the face of trial and tribulation.

Writing from a prison cell in Rome, he must have relived all that had happened to him during those eventful years. He knew that his days were numbered, but he gloried in what had happened to him and how his life had been changed. Surely he recalled how he had started out relentless in his determination to persecute the Christians, and how on that lonely Damascan road he had a vision which resulted in a changed life. Surely he could feel even now the sting that came when a stone had been thrown in hatred at him and had left an ugly scar on his face. Then there were the lashes and the rods which had cut his back. He could never forget the storm-tossed days on an ocean voyage and the shipwreck which had almost cost him his life.

But facing the executioners who would soon knock at his door, he could write from his prison cell: *"I know the one in whom I have put my trust."*

He did not question why God allowed it to happen any more than he questioned Stephen's stoning, which he had witnessed in Jerusalem before his conversion. He did not demand that God should give him reasons for all that was unwanted which had come his way; he simply trusted. Paul knew that God had his best interest at heart and that there was nothing too good to believe about him.

What a lesson for us today! Is it not the mark of true friendship to need no explanation for all that happens, but in spite of everything still to trust and love a friend? When we really trust another, we know that even if we do not understand why an incident occurs, we believe in our friend because we know that friend was acting in our best interest.

Now there are many questions which we cannot answer about God and God's world. Many things happen to us which may seem unjust; many sorrows, hard to bear, come our way; many disappointments overtake us unexpectedly along the way. At times we are apt to blame God. "Why did this have to happen to me?" we cry out in our anguish. "Why have you forsaken me?"

We believe that though we are not freed completely from trouble, *yet we are saved in trouble.* In other words God offers help in seeing us through. Paul puts it like this in Romans 8:28: "We know that all things work together for good for those who love God, who are called according to his purpose."

Let us take this lesson from Paul and emulate his faith by placing in God a confidence so great that, regardless of what may happen to us, we still will love and trust God and are able to say: "I know the one in whom I have put my trust, and I am sure that he is able to guard until that day what I have entrusted to him."

Hymns: "My Jesus, as Thou Wilt!"
"Blessed Assurance"

Scripture: II Timothy 1:1-14

PRAYER

Most gracious God, whose greatness is beyond our conception, we pause today to acknowledge our unworthiness. Judge us, we pray, by your great mercy and not according to our merits. Coming into your holy presence makes us conscious of our feebleness and sinfulness, for in your light our lives are blighted with scars. Yet we would remember the promise of your Son, who assured forgiveness to all who repent and return to you.

> Forgive us for doubting moments when your promises lie hidden in our minds;
> Forgive us of selfish ambitions unbecoming servants of so great a God;

Forgive us of jealousies which canker the soul;
Forgive us for lack of faith when darkness makes us afraid;
Forgive us for slowness to see the virtues of others and
quickness to see their faults.

Stab us awake to our many needs. Drive us to our knees in penitence for all our failures and raise us up as your new servants, through Jesus Christ our Lord. AMEN.

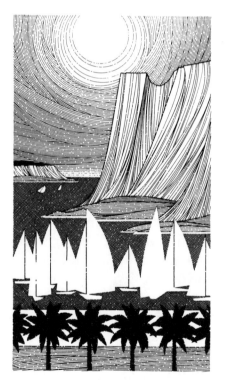

FAITH IS MORE THAN BELIEF

Many times in the years gone by young men visiting their homes for the last time before going overseas had in their possession sealed orders. They did not know their destination.

In a real sense we all sail forth each day under sealed orders. We know not what the day may bring forth. Life is quick with mystery.

How shall we meet it—with faith or fear? That is the question. To meet it with fear means failure; it takes all meaning from life, robbing it of joy. To meet it with faith adds hope to life; it gives joy to living.

Faith is more than belief about God; it is trust in God. Real faith goes deeper than mere belief. We can believe in something without giving ourselves to it. But real faith goes beyond faith to trust. It is an act of the will. To have faith we must have an abiding trust.

Let us contrast the attitudes of two men. Both believe in God; both believe in immortality; both believe in the goodness of God. Both attest to a firm belief. But here is the difference: one has a deep faith, a trust, a dependence upon that which he believes to be true. The other lacks this trust. The first, when he is sick, is not fretful. Facing an operation, he does so in trust, in poise, in confidence. The other faces illness as a child. He is frightened; he is fearful. He cannot bear bad news. His belief does not extend to a firm faith which is trust. One faces death with confidence and with hope. He rests his life on the "everlasting arms." He trusts Christ. The other, facing the uncertainty of illness, becomes a man torn with fears. He lacks deep faith.

So to have real faith you must have trust. Faith goes beyond belief to trust. Philosophy deals with belief; religion deals with trust. One is an assent of the mind; the other, an act of the will. Belief is theology; trust is religion. Trust, of course, cannot exist without belief.

It is when belief moves over into trust and dependence that men and women are willing to give their lives in devotion and sacrifice to Christ. It is when belief in ideas becomes trust that missionaries journey into far-off fields.

Jesus sensed our need to really trust. When in Luke 12:28 he said, "If God so clothes the grass of the field, which is alive today and tomorrow is thrown into the oven, how much more will he clothe you—you of little faith!" he seemed to be asking these questions: Do you merely believe in God, or do you believe in him enough to give your life to his keeping? Do you believe in God's promises enough to trust your life to him in the unknown future? Do you go out each day in confidence? Do you live unafraid, knowing that always about your life is everlasting mercy? Do you live a fretful life or one of inner peace?

Jesus knew that faith must operate in stormy weather as well as on sunny days. But too many of us have a fair-weather faith. We believe when all is well, but our beliefs are shaken when trouble comes.

God is good, we reason, when the sun is shining and life is running in gear, but when a storm arises, when a war reaches into our homes, then it is that our shallow belief crumbles unless our faith is grounded in a deathless trust.

The only basis for a faith that sustains is trust in a God who cares, who is close to us, who is always there, who always seeks to help us, whose plans for our lives exceed our fondest hopes. On such a living, moving, accessible Being do we have a faith that propels.

What does a faith like that do for us? Radiant lives all around testify to its fruits. It frees our minds from fears of the future for work with tasks at hand. It sends us out in confidence. It starts us onward into each day with a sense of adventure; a sense that this is God's world and we are the children of God working in it.

It gives us a sense of mission. We become people with assignments, with jobs to do for God. When a person loses this sense of mission it is the loss of one of the greatest driving forces in life. It frees us from hurried nervousness, a cause for so much illness today. It centers our inner life around one Master and saves us from splitting our lives by trying to go in all directions at once. In short, it becomes for us a saving faith.

Hymns: "O Love That Wilt Not Let Me Go"
"There's a Wideness in God's Mercy"

Scripture: Romans 8:14-28

PRAYER

Eternal God, you are our refuge and strength. With grateful hearts we praise you. We know you are near to guard and to guide. Even when we are unaware of your presence, you reach out to us and bless us.

Here this day we rest our fears into your keeping. We know that without your strength life's loads would be too much for us and life's fears would cause us to stumble. Facing life with you, we find that our moments of uncertainty turn to hours of adventure, and our times of suffering become opportunities for knowing you better.

Give us this day a clearer grasp of the things which belong unto our peace, through Jesus Christ our Lord. AMEN.

GRATITUDE HEALS A BROKEN HEART

All of us find ourselves at one time or another faced with sorrow and grief. What can we do when we lose those we love?

There are three things to suggest. First, let us remember that life is a fragile thing, and that we all soon follow those who slip from our midst.

Addison in his Meditations in Westminster Abbey has a word of comfort for us:

"When I look upon the tombs of the great, every emotion of envy dies in me; when I read the epitaphs of the beautiful, every inordinate desire goes out; when I meet with the grief of parents upon a tombstone, my heart melts with compassion; when I see the tombs of the parents themselves, I consider the vanity of grieving for those whom we must quickly follow; when I see kings lying by those who deposed them, when I consider rival wits placed side by side, or the holy men that divided the world with their contests and disputes, I reflect with sorrow and astonishment on the little competitions, factions and debates of mankind."

So, remembering that we follow those who leave us and through our faith can look forward to a blessed reunion brings a measure of comfort to us.

Again, to busy ourselves with work can help us through the valley of sorrow. The other day a friend of mine who had lost a young son through a dreadful accident, said to me, "You know, after Jerry was killed, my husband and I busied ourselves with our work. We visited our people from morning till night; sharing their problems helped us with ours. I don't know how we would have gotten through those days had it not been for our work." How many people have had the anguish of sorrow lessened by work! If the days are past when you had a daily job to go to, consider volunteering. Many places have need for those who will lend a listening ear.

Finally, it is through gratitude that we find our best antidote for sorrow. Even in the midst of our tears we can discover so much for which we have to be grateful. Dwelling here helps to heal our wounds.

Recently, where there had been long illness and suffering, a loved one who had been standing by in tender care said, "I know I have so much to be thankful for. And remembering God's mercy and blessings has helped me stand these days." How true this is!

Whether we are faced with bereavement, disappointment, or joy, let us make it a habit to be grateful to God for the boundless love and goodness expressed in our lives in so many ways. It is good to "count our many blessings, name them one by one." Gratitude lights a lonely way. Gratitude helps to heal a broken heart.

Shakespeare put it like this: "God's goodness hath been great to thee. Let never day nor night unhallowed pass, but still remember what the Lord hath done."

A person confessed that he would never forget the beauty and serenity that possessed the life of his grandmother. Her long years were fraught with many trials and tribulations, but her life was like a song. Always in her heart and frequently upon her lips were these words of the Psalmist: "Bless the Lord, O my soul: and all that is within me, bless his holy name. Bless the Lord, O my soul, and forget not all his benefits."

Hymns: "Near to the Heart of God"
          "Lord, for Tomorrow and Its Needs"

Scripture: Psalm 63:1-7

PRAYER

O eternal One, Comforter of all, draw especially near to all whose hearts are filled with sadness over the loss of a loved one. Beyond their tears help them to know there is life that will never end. In their sadness help them know that you understand. In their loneliness make them conscious of your great love. In their grief draw them closer to you.

Help them bear bravely the anguish of these hours. Fill the vacancy of their hearts with your abiding presence, which links us to those who pass beyond. Grant that we may rest our fears in your hands, trusting in your promises and waiting for the day when we shall be joined together in your eternal home, through Jesus Christ, our Lord. Amen.

WORRY—WRECKER OF LIFE

Worry wrecks more lives than wars! Let us see what it does to life.

In the first place, worry is a wrecker of life. It is a destroyer of happiness. Life for most people would be happy and satisfying if they could overcome worry. In a real sense worry is the interest you pay on trouble before it comes. Many times the things we worry about never happen.

All of us have had the experience of fretting over something we were afraid would happen, only to find that it never happened. We have crossed bridges before we got to them and often have discovered that there were no bridges to cross. As a wrecker of life, worry not only destroys happiness but is a breaker of health. We are told that one out of ten people in the United States will have a nervous breakdown, and many of these breakdowns will be caused by worry and emotional conflicts.

Again, as a wrecker of life worry incapacitates us for work. All of us have had the experience of being worried, and we know how it slows us down because our minds are otherwise engaged. In a real sense folks do not work themselves into graves; they worry themselves into them.

The big question, then, is, How are we to handle our worries; how can we overcome them? Someone has well said, "All the Declaration of Independence mentions is the *pursuit* of happiness. You have to catch up with it for yourself."

For one thing, it is good to ask, *Just why are we worrying?* Get all the facts. What is the origin of the worry? Where did it come from? Is it real or imaginary? Many times we discover that to run worries down often leads to their disappearance. Worry frequently is fear of failure, a concern lest we fail to measure up to what is expected of us. We worry about what people will say.

Not only does it help to get the facts, but then we should *do something about them.* Our worries should be met with action. Action, even if it is unwise action, is better than living under fear, which tends to breed indecision. Brooding is the worst thing we can do.

And then, let us try to *live one day at a time.* Do the task at hand. To worry over what must be done next year, to worry about the next pain, will only lead to more and more stress and worry.

Finally, the greatest antidote for worry is to *commit life each day into the hands of a loving and kind God.* Such trust banishes worry; strong faith drives it out. Take verses such as these into your daily round and worry will be crowded out: "My help comes from the Lord, who made heaven and earth" (Psalm 121:2). "I can do all things through him who strengthens me" (Philippians 4:13). "Christ Jesus has made me his own" (Philippians 3:12).

Hymns: "How Firm a Foundation"
    "God Is My Strong Salvation"

Scripture: Psalm 121

PRAYER

Eternal God, creator of all life, ruler of all nature, source of all strength, we give you thanks for your great love toward us and toward all people everywhere. Into your holy presence we come, lifting our common supplications. You know our needs, our fears, our anxieties, our unanswered perplexities. The burdens we carry are known by you. The heartaches which disturb us are not foreign to your knowledge.

Keep us still that we may listen.

Keep us believing that we may know.

Keep us pure that we may see.

Keep us brave that we may venture.

Keep us close that we may walk in confidence.

Send us out, O God, with the assurance that life with all its fears can be faced in victory with you. AMEN.

GIVE IT TIME

We are impatient people. We want what we want, when we want it and that is usually now. We are not prone to wait. But whether we recognize it or not, time is a great boon to us. Time helps heal the wounds of sorrow; it is needed in all growth; it helps us to forget; it can clarify our thinking and rightly direct our action.

All of us have had the experience of facing a problem which seemed insurmountable. No matter how hard we tried we could not find the right set of answers with which to solve it. We may have lost sleep over the problem. It may have brought to us great despair. We saw no way out. Then we waited, and the pieces began to fit together. Light came out of darkness, and a new pattern began to take shape. New ideas overtook us. Finally, the solution came.

Byron once wrote:

> Time! the corrector where our judgments err;
> the test of truth, and love; the sole philosopher.

Of course we can make of time an excuse not to decide, an evasion of duty, or an unwillingness to face or accept what must be done. But most of us are in danger of rushing in, of demanding now what only time can bring. Faced as we often are with indecision and the frustration that it can bring, we are apt to get it over with and decide hastily when we should wait and give it time.

Surely time is one of the tools of God—to bring healing, to permit growth, to open doors of understanding. Frequently in our scriptures we read these words: "until the time comes." For example we read in Luke 13:35, "You will not see me until the time comes when you say, 'Blessed is the one who comes in the name of the Lord.'"

In John 16:12 we have these words of Jesus: "I still have many things to say to you, but you cannot bear them now." Jesus is saying here that time is needed for preparation, for understanding of the truth of God. He is speaking here in his farewell discourse of the frankness with which he has shared the insights he has learned from his Father. But he is telling them that they are not yet spiritually mature enough for all that God has in store for them.

So, let us be grateful for time which ripens and which brings forth readiness and fullness. When we are faced with a problem, these are not idle words when someone tells us to "sleep on it," for sleep "knits up the ravell'd sleave of care." The morning not only ushers in a new day but heralds new wisdom which only time can bring.

Hymns: "Love Divine, All Loves Excelling"
          "Be Still, My Soul"

Scripture: John 16:1-16

PRAYER

Eternal God, in whom we live and move and have our being, with grateful hearts we lift our prayer to you.

We thank you for this lovely day and for every suggestion of your presence in our midst. We are grateful for this hour in which we may hear your voice and feel your nearness.

Give us a vision of life at its best. Lift us upward that we may see your truth, and open our hearts that we may receive your word. Be with all who are in distress today, the sorrowing, the suffering, the overworked, the unemployed, the sin-sick, and the lost. Bring your healing love to give release. Take from us despair and give us hope, through Jesus Christ our Lord. AMEN.

FAITH'S ANSWER TO FEAR

Fear is common to all people. Some fears are born in us, but most of them begin in early childhood, and all of them can influence our lives for good or ill.

If you are afraid, remember that you are not by yourself and that fear is one of life's most common maladies. It can incapacitate us for work and for joyous living. One cannot be in complete control of one's faculties nor be at one's best when encumbered with fear. It saps energies needed for constructive purposes and sometimes paralyzes us.

Yet fear is not always a villain. On the contrary it may be a benevolent force making us aware of physical dangers. It can be a red-light signal, a "stop, look, and listen" sign of impending doom ahead. Fear keeps us from being hit by a train. It discourages us from living in unsanitary conditions, from disobeying doctor's orders. In a sense we are blessed by the capacity to know fear. All inventions are in a measure by-products of fears and worries. Fear has often been the stimulus to growth, the goad to invention.

But there is a difference between desirable and undesirable fear; a little is necessary, but excessive amounts distort our whole future. So our business in one sense is not to get rid of fear, but to harness it.

What, then, is faith's answer to fear? Four words are suggestive as an answer: *knowledge, action, purpose,* and *dependence.* Expose your fears to knowledge. Drag them out into the light of day and see them as they really are. Many times we have real and genuine reasons for being afraid. On the other hand, many of our fears are imaginary. We shake the bear and find it to be a bush.

Often our fears will evaporate after we have taken a good look. They look so grotesque in the darkness and so small in the light of day. Most of the things people fear never happen.

Every person should ask, "What am I afraid of?" "Why am I disturbed?" Then give an honest answer. Knowing the situation may bring bad news, but at least we can know where we are and the thing with which we are dealing.

Our fears should be met with action. It is often good to do the thing you fear. If you fear ill health, go to a doctor. If you dread loneliness, share another's suffering. If you fear to be around certain people, deliberately go around them. Many times doing the thing we fear helps to conquer it.

We know the value of dependence, the added strength and courage a companion gives us when we are on a strange and dangerous journey. We know what it is to have someone standing by when we face sorrow and suffering. Greater than all human companionship is divine companionship. People who believe in God can accomplish more than those who do not. They trust God to care for them. Such trust releases power for achievement and throws all effort into work without the hampering of fear. This is faith's answer to fear.

Hymns: "More Love to Thee, O Christ"
      "Blessed Assurance"

Scripture: Romans 5:1-8

PRAYER

O God, in whose hands our lives rest and in whose providence we spend our days, there are so many mysteries that baffle our minds. There are so many questions we cannot answer. There are so many problems to make us doubt. We do not know and understand all we want to know. Our faith is not as firm as we want it to be. But, O God, we do know enough of your goodness, your forgiveness, your love to make us want to hold fast to you. We do know that:

You have been so gracious and you are One to whom we owe life itself.

Your hand has been upon our shoulders, guiding our faltering footsteps.

Your presence has surrounded our being, bringing comfort in hours of distress.

Your love has forgiven our sinful ways, offering new beginnings; and your strength has upheld us, reinforcing us in our weakness.

Continue, we pray, to illumine our darkness and displace our doubts with your assurance. In his name, which is above all names, we pray. AMEN.

ACCEPT WHAT CANNOT BE CHANGED

Reinhold Niebuhr wrote this prayer:

> God grant me the serenity
> To accept the things I cannot change;
> The courage to change the things I can;
> And the wisdom to distinguish the one from the other.

Let us think together about one phrase from this lesson, which deals with acceptance. All of us are confronted in life with situations we'd like to change, but cannot. What are we going to do with these situations? That is the question.

We can give or "bend like a tree planted by the water" with the storms of life, or we can resist and break. This is the rule by which Jesus lived. It did not make of him a coward or a weakling, but enabled him to gain power over himself and his world. It is the Christian approach to life.

In the first place *we must learn to accept ourselves*. Rather than feeling sorry for ourselves and the limitations which life has given us, let us accept them and remember the words: "You are the children of God."

In the second place, we must learn to *accept people as they are*. Remembering our own faults and failures, let us be charitable toward others.

In a certain garage the serviceman makes entries in his daybook in such a way as to identify owners, such as "Mrs. Ellis won't start"; "Something wrong with Mr. Pitt's wiring."

Now, there are a lot of folks who appear to us to be in need of repairs, but it will save us many a headache if we will accept them as they are, knowing that we, too, have our bumped fenders and run-down batteries. Jesus looked at people and accepted them as they were, felt sorry for their faults, and loved them as brother and sister, children of God.

Again, we must learn to *accept situations which cannot be altered*. In other words we must learn to cooperate with the inevitable. The late King George V had these famed words hanging on the wall of his library: "Teach me neither to cry for the moon nor over spilt milk." But my, how hard that is to do! It is one of the toughest lessons we have to learn. Sooner or later we all have to learn to accept situations in life which cannot be altered.

All of this does not mean that we are to be weak and cowardly as we face life. It does not mean that we are to be filled with despair. It does not mean that we are to bow down to all adversities that come our way. That is mere fatalism. We must fight as long as we can to save a situation, but when there is nothing more that we can do, wisdom tells us to accept it as a fact.

But let us remember, too, that God's plans and purposes are not dependent upon their fulfillment here. He has an eternity in which to work them out.

Hymns: "Jesus Calls Us"
"O Jesus, I Have Promised"

Scripture: Philippians 4:1-13

PRAYER

O God, forgive us for letting life's annoyances cripple our spirits. Unexpected interruptions, necessary details, and the day's routine have marred our dispositions. To cover up our own weaknesses, we have blamed them on others. To find release from explosions within, we have said things we should not have said. To give expression to our impatience, we have turned our anger loose on objects nearby. For our loss of control we are deeply repentant; for our lack of inner steadiness we ask pardon. Fill us with a portion of your everflowing patience and grant us a new chance to redeem our lives from unworthiness. Give our souls calmness sufficient for life's unrest. In the face of irritating circumstances, give us steadfastness and control. Through Jesus Christ our Lord. AMEN.

IDEALS AND THE POWER TO SEE THEM THROUGH

Every one of us has a code of conduct by which daily life is measured. For some to follow that code has become an unconscious habit; it is indeed part of us. Yet, I am thinking today how often you and I feel that we need something more which will help us follow that which we know to be right.

We know in general what is right, but how hard it is at times to follow the right. Certainly the complexities of modern life have forced us to reduce our religion to something simple to which we may hold. Some time ago, a man stated that his religion was following the Golden Rule, and he thought that was enough. High code? Yes! But do we not need something more which will help us follow that code?

Younger people sometimes feel that ethics and philosophy are sufficient for living, that religion is necessary only for the ignorant and superstitious. We can tell them this, however, from our view from the later years: "Yes, to be sure you have a code of conduct, a system of morality, a high set of ideals. But can you give yourself completely to a set of ideals? Yes, you have a code. But what will give you the power to follow that code? You have perhaps gleaned from the ages what humankind has found to be the best way to live, but what will give you courage and strength needed to live that type of life?"

It is here that religion comes in, for it offers not only a high system of ideals but also a source of strength and power needed to see them through. And when religion is viewed only as a set of ideals, then it ceases to become a religion and remains only a formula or a set of rules.

Have you ever felt that your religion was a burden to you, keeping you from enjoying life, and that you would like to throw it overboard? When we feel that way, it means just this—we have a high set of ideals and little or no power to see them through. Ideals without incentive or motivating power are like cars without gasoline, lighting fixtures without electricity.

A high sense of duty, yes, but with it a high level of power. For many years so much of our preaching has been centered on the ethics of Jesus—his way of life, his high standards of

71

living—and this has helped to reduce our faith in a large measure to a matter of conduct. We need not only to say "behave" but also "behold." "Behold the Lamb of God." The greatness of Jesus rests not only in his high ethical teachings but more in that power which enabled him to live those teachings and in his power to see them through.

His uniqueness lay in his relationship to God. The way Jesus lived and his principles in life were the result of his close fellowship with the Father. He lived as he did because God gave him the power to do so. Before a hard day or after the cares and problems of the multitude had pressed upon him until nightfall, he would go apart in quiet and meditation to be alone with God. And after each such hour he came back a new person. He had not only a high sense of duty but also a high level of power.

How we need this today! For too long we have left God out of the picture. We have forgotten that God is the sovereign ruler of this universe, that God is not only creator but sustainer as well. We have thought for long that we could run our own lives and the affairs of the world without God's help. We must return to God.

When we think of God as we know him in Christ, let us think not so much of the fact that he left us the Sermon on the Mount, important as it is, but rather that he left himself for us. On that last day with his disciples he did not say, "I leave my sermons and my code with you," but, "I leave myself. I will always be with you."

Hymns: "I Want a Principle Within"
  "Savior, More than Life to Me"

Scripture: Matthew 28:16-20

PRAYER

Eternal God, you have been our dwelling place in all generations. Before the mountains were brought forth, before you formed the earth, even from everlasting to everlasting, you are God.

We come before you this day unworthy of your love; we come stained by temptations which so easily beset us; we come feeling

72

need of you—your power, your strength, and your forgiveness. You know us better than we know ourselves. You know our need and are standing ready to help us. Take us this day and lift us upward. Strengthen our steps. Enlarge our visions. Quicken our hopes. Purify our motives. Remind us of the things which do not change, and secure us to life's unfading treasures. In the name and in the spirit of Christ, we pray. AMEN.

SHEEP STILL NEED A SHEPHERD

Several summers ago a minister was in South Dakota visiting friends who owned a sheep ranch. They took him one day across the range where the sheep were grazing. As he left this pastoral scene, knowing that sheep still need a shepherd, he thought of David's Twenty-third Psalm, in which David likens people to sheep and the Lord to a shepherd.

It was natural that David would use such figures of speech and natural, too, that Jesus would use the figure of a shepherd's care in watching over his sheep in speaking of God's love and care.

The Shepherd's Psalm has "dried many a tear and supplied the mold into which many hearts have poured their faith." It is the utterance of personal trust in the Lord, darkened by no fears or complaints, asking for nothing but grateful for such care.

In this psalm of quiet trust the one central thought is expanded in two kindred images—that of the shepherd and the host.

In the first image, God sustains us. God is our guide on the journey of life. *"The Lord is my shepherd."* How much meaning is packed into those melodious works! We see God as our guide protecting us from evil and harm.

Even if *"I walk through the valley of the shadow of death, I will fear no evil: for thou art with me; thy rod and thy staff they comfort me."** The valley of the shadow is not necessarily death, but moments of darkness and despair, hours of loneliness and disappointment. But even in death we are never alone. God is with us; his rod and his staff are our stays. To the sheep out in the wilderness, the shepherd and his staff protect them from harm.

So the journey of life is not always bright and smooth, but sometimes plunges us down into grim canyons where no sunbeams reach. Even so, that anticipation can be met with calm. "Thou art with me" is enough.

The second image we have is that of host. God not only

---

*Scripture quotations for this meditation are from the King James Version.

sustains us, but entertains us. We are really guests enjoying God's hospitality. God even gives us a banquet.

"The Lord is my shepherd; I shall not want. He maketh me to lie down in green pastures: he leadeth me beside the still waters." Here the Psalmist tells of the tender care of God for childhood, when we are only lambs. A lamb is too timid to drink of rough waters. Thus, "he leadeth me beside still waters." "Goodness and mercy" follow us all the way until at last we are in God's house.

Then we find the spirit of Jesus in the psalm. Listen to his words: "I am the good shepherd: the good shepherd gives his life for the sheep"; "My sheep hear my voice, and I know them, and they follow me."

For us Jesus Christ is the Good Shepherd. His spirit is let loose in the world. He is alive forevermore. We see him going in search of the lost sheep, yearning for each one to be in the Father's fold.

Indeed, "The Lord is my shepherd!"

Hymns: "Savior, Like a Shepherd Lead Us"
"He's the Savior of My Soul"

Scripture: Psalm 23

PRAYER

Eternal God, in whom there is no darkness, and from whom we find light for life's journey, with gratitude we come into your holy presence today. We cannot fully know you or completely understand you; yet what we know inspires us to love and worship you.

We rejoice that you have made yourself known to us through your son, Jesus Christ. Help us to find in him today, through the Holy Spirit, strength and power for our feeble lives. We rejoice that you watch every event of our mortal lives. We know that nothing escapes your notice. Renew within our hearts the faith that all things work together for good to them that love you.

Grant to every one of us today the help and strength we need. Fill our fearful lives with confident trust. Quicken our faltering steps to a steady pace. Flood our sorrowful heart with abiding joy and lift our lonely souls with your comforting presence, through Christ our Lord. AMEN.

THE UTMOST FOR THE HIGHEST

In O. Henry's short story *The Gift of the Magi*, we have the gripping narrative of two young lovers at Christmastime. Their love expressed itself with each trying to give the finest gift to the other. They had little money, and so the wife sold her lovely hair in order to buy a watch fob for her husband.

He had a watch which had been handed down from one generation to the next, from his grandfather's time, and he had planned to pass it on to his son, if they had one. It was his most prized possession. But he sold it in order to buy a beautiful set of combs to adorn his wife's hair.

As the gifts were exchanged, a sense of bewilderment overtook the couple, and then in good humor they rushed into each other's arms, laughing and crying. In spite of their disappointment they realized that each had given the utmost to his and her highest affection. What a priceless gift!

As we turn our thoughts this Christmas to the story of the Wise Men bringing their gifts to the Christ child, we can see how this story relates to these men bringing gold, frankincense, and myrrh. They brought their best—the utmost for the highest!

One brought gold, which can represent gifts of substance. This is mentioned first perhaps because our gifts of substance are so hard to give freely and gladly. Yet, much of the strife of life comes with the clutching of things, holding on to the material.

Unless we bring our substance and lay it at God's feet, then our substance takes the place of life itself. Bringing our gold is recognizing that God has given us all that we have and that we are merely stewards for a little while.

When the Wise Man brought his gold, he fell down and worshiped the Christ Child. Could it be that unless we bring our substance to God, we cannot really worship? His giving recognized a basic principle in life; namely, we need to give more than God needs what we have to give.

Another Wise Man brought frankincense, which can represent wisdom and influence. Here is wisdom as well as substance bowing down before the babe. These men represent the learning of the ages, the wisdom of the world. They were the scientists of their time.

This is a symbol for us today of the need for knowledge to gain direction and purpose in its use. Real wisdom is more than knowledge. Knowledge is the accumulation of facts; wisdom is the interpretation of facts. Knowledge is culled from textbooks; wisdom comes out of life.

A third brought myrrh. Myrrh was used as an embalming fluid, and thus can *represent for us sorrow and suffering.* This is the hardest and bitterest to give to Christ. It is easier to harbor our suffering and sorrow in bitter protest.

George A. Buttrick says, "The reason why sorrow hardens one man and melts another is just that the one man keeps his sorrow selfishly and the other offers it in oblation."

So when the Christmas season moves toward the New Year, let us offer God our gold, the substance of our lives; our frankincense, the inner treasure of our thoughts; and our myrrh, the suffering and sorrow of our hearts.

Hymns: "O Come, All Ye Faithful"
        "We Three Kings of Orient Are"

Scripture: Matthew 2:1-12

PRAYER

O God, from the hurry of a busy week we pause lifting our eyes from the temporal scene to catch a glimpse of eternity. In the fevered rush of these days we would be still for a little while and remind ourselves why we celebrate Christmas.

Forbid that the joy of Christmas would come only from the pale reflection of colored lights that soon burn out and from trimmed trees that die of thirst. Forbid that we should be so preoccupied with the exchange of gifts that we forget life's supreme gift. Let us not become so enamored with the things of this world that we forget our taste for spiritual things.

Help us to find gladness for our hearts because the light of divine love came down at Christmastime and became a light that will never go out. No sadness can rob us of its joy, no sorrow can take it away. We find cheer at this season in family circles when we mean more to each other, and when we try to stop time and hold these fleeting minutes.

Bless us this year as we gather around our firesides and as our love is made to glow with your love in our hearts.

Comfort those who mourn and suffer this day, and may they in their sorrow find you as one who heals our wounds and shares our cares.

Over the tumult of our world and the noise of the marketplace, may the voice of Christ ring clear and true, speaking the word of peace and reconciliation to our wayward ways. AMEN.